D0604515

JOANNA COLE

THE HUMAN BODY

HOW WE EVOLVED

ILLUSTRATED BY

WALTER GAFFNEY-KESSELL

— AND —

JUAN CARLOS BARBERIS

WILLIAM MORROW & COMPANY, INC./NEW YORK

Acknowledgment

The author wishes to thank Ian Tattersall of the Department of Anthropology of the American Museum of Natural History for his helpful reading and critique of the manuscript and illustrations.

Text copyright © 1987 by Joanna Cole

Illustrations on pages 4–5, 8 (boy), 10–11, 32, 33, 40, 41, 42–43, 48–49, 50–51, 56–57, 58, and 59 copyright © 1987 by Juan Carlos Barberis
All other illustrations copyright © 1987 by Walter Gaffney-Kessell

All rights reserved. No part of this book
may be reproduced or utilized in any
form or by any means, electronic or mechanical,
including photocopying, recording or by
any information storage and retrieval system,
without permission in writing from the Publisher.
Inquiries should be addressed to
William Morrow and Company, Inc.,
105 Madison Avenue,
New York, NY 10016.

Printed in the United States of America.
1 2 3 4 5 6 7 8 9 10

Library of Congress Cataloging-in-Publication Data
Cole, Joanna.
The human body.
Summary: Traces the development of man, from early
prehistoric ancestors to the modern tool-user who walks
upright.
1. Body, Human—Juvenile literature. [1. Man,
Prehistoric. 2. Evolution] I. Gaffney-Kessell,
Walter, ill. II. Barberis, Juan Carlos, ill. III. Title.
QM27.C65 1987   612   86-23679
ISBN 0-688-06719-0
ISBN 0-688-06720-4 (lib. bdg.)

To Michael Stone

Imagine that a visitor from another planet came to earth and visited a zoo. It looked at the giraffe's long neck and the elephant's trunk. But then it noticed the *other* animals at the zoo—the human animals. It thought these were the most interesting and unusual of all. For humans are very different from other animals.

We walk on two legs, instead of going on four, like almost all other mammals.

We wear clothes because, unlike most other mammals, we are not covered with a coat of fur.

And most unusual of all, we are so amazingly intelligent. Not only do we come to the zoo to look at the other animals,

we are the ones who got the idea of having a zoo in the first place. We built it, captured the animals, and are now in charge of feeding and caring for them. For all this, we use tools and machines made by humans. We even talk among ourselves about whether it is right to keep other animals locked up.

Yet, as different as humans are from other animals, we are part of the animal world. Humans belong to a group called the primates, which also includes lemurs, monkeys, and apes. Our closest living relatives are chimpanzees and gorillas, which are both apes.

Like all other animals, humans evolved, or developed, from earlier forms of life. Looking at how we evolved can tell us a lot about why we are the way we are.

Primates.

About 15 million years ago, our ancestors were probably apelike tree dwellers that lived in what is now Africa. These primate ancestors had evolved in the forest and were well suited to life there. They found a steady supply of fruits and leaves to eat in the trees. And they could escape from enemies by swinging rapidly away through the branches.

Although these tree dwellers were not exactly like the apes we know today, they were more like apes than humans. They probably had low foreheads and small brains, compared to those of modern humans or even modern apes. On the ground, they probably went on all fours.

Ancestor of apes and humans.

Then, about 11 million years ago, the environment began to change. Gradually the forests were replaced by open woodlands and huge stretches of grassland called savannas. By around 5 million years ago, some forest-dwelling primates had ventured out to live on the plains.

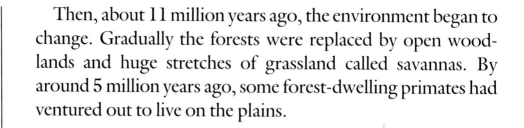

Life on the savanna was very different from forest life. Food was harder to get, and there were dangerous meat-eating animals all around.

The former tree dwellers were not very well equipped to defend themselves. They were small compared to many other plains animals. If they were surprised by a predator, they could not run very fast to escape. And on the savanna there were few places to hide.

First primates on African savanna, 5 million years ago.

The best defense for primates on the savanna was to see danger before it got too close. In an open area, the taller an animal is, the farther it can see and the safer it is. An animal whose eyes are two feet off the ground can see six miles away. But eyes that are five feet above the ground can see *fifteen* miles away!

Upright primates could also use their arms to carry food and infants, and they could spot food at a distance. Standing upright protected primates in another way: an upright animal looks bigger, which makes predators less likely to attack.

Humanlike
primates,
3.5 million
years ago.

On the plains, those primate species that were more upright
were better at gathering food and protecting themselves from
danger. Their offspring had a better chance of living to grow
up than the offspring of less upright primates. By about 3.5 to
4 million years ago, a species of prehuman had evolved that
walked on two legs, as we do today.

Scientists have found fossil bones of these early upright creatures. The scientific name for their species is *Australopithecus afarensis*, but they are often called australopithecines (os-TRAL-oh-PITH-uh-seens).

The most complete fossil skeleton of an australopithecine is that of a female. The scientists who found it named her Lucy.

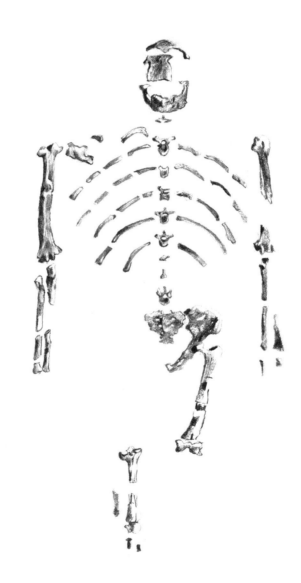

Fossil skeleton of Lucy, Australopithecus afarensis.

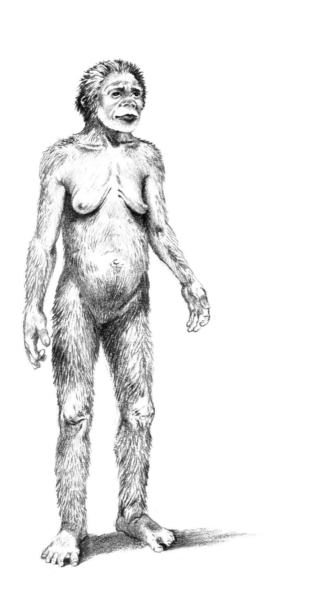

Lucy is the oldest primate fossil skeleton that is more like a human than an ape. For this reason Lucy is called a hominid (HAH-min-id), which means a primate belonging to the human family.

Lucy's brain was much smaller than a modern human's. But we can tell that she walked upright from the shape of her hip-bones, or pelvis.

Lucy was a humanlike primate. Lucy's pelvis is more like a human's than an ape's.

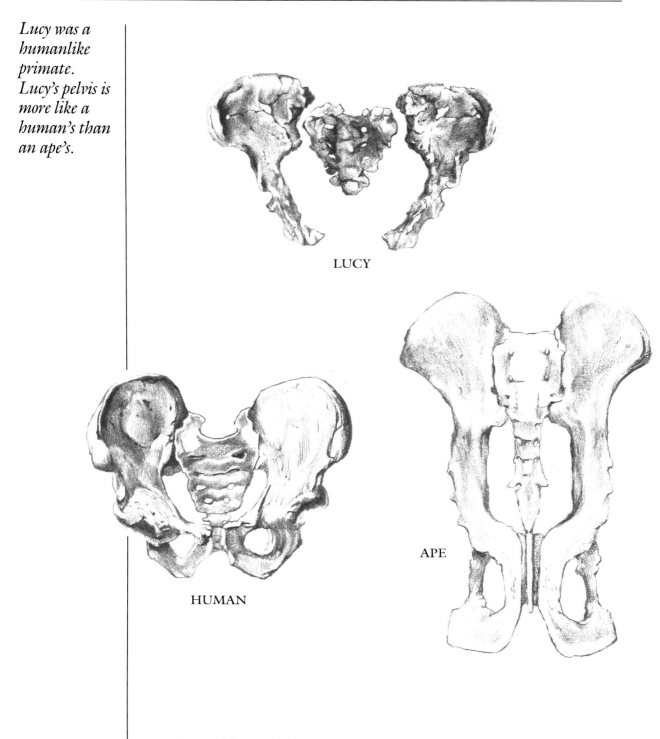

LUCY

HUMAN

APE

The shape of the pelvis is important because most of the walking muscles are attached to it. Lucy's pelvis is short and wide, like the pelvis of a modern human rather than the pelvis of a modern ape, which is long and narrow.

Modern apes are able to walk on two legs, but because of the shape of their pelvis and thighbones, they can do so only for short distances. When apes walk upright, the knees and hips are always bent. The feet are set far apart, so the body weight shifts from side to side.

In the modern human—and in Lucy—the feet are close together under the middle of the body, so the weight shifts only a small amount. Unlike apes, we don't "rock" as we stride efficiently forward.

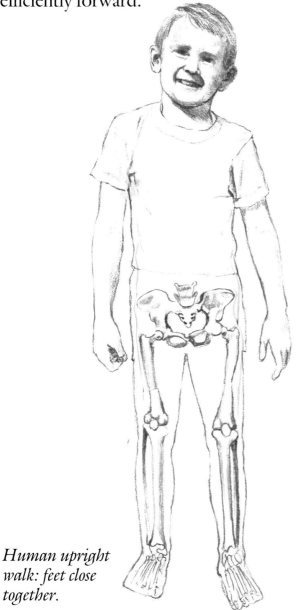

Human upright walk: feet close together.

Ape's upright walk: feet wide apart.

The structure of the foot is also important in upright walking. The big toe of our early ancestors was not a grasping toe like that of a tree-dwelling primate—a long toe that sticks out like a thumb on the side of the foot. Instead, their big toe was short, and it pointed forward with the other toes.

LUCY

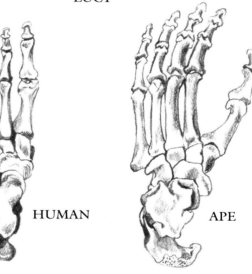

HUMAN   APE

The australopithecine foot is a walking foot like a human's, not a grasping foot like an ape's.

A big toe like ours is the "motor" that propels the body forward. With each stride, the weight of the body falls first on the heel. Then it is shifted to the outside edge of the foot, then to the ball of the foot. Finally the big toe pushes the body ahead. The small toes are used for balancing.

The pelvis and foot bones of australopithecines tell us that our ancestors began walking upright very early in their history—long before the evolution of larger brains and probably before much use of tools and weapons.

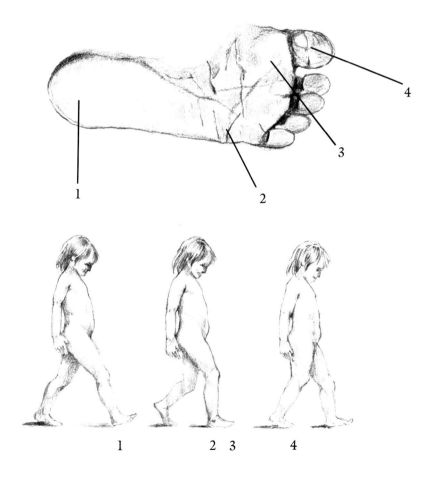

When you take a step your weight falls on your . . .
(1) heel,
(2) edge of foot,
(3) ball of foot,
(4) big toe.

20

Because there are no fossils of fur, we do not know for sure when our ancestors lost their heavy coat. We do know that humans have the same *number* of hairs as other primates—such as gorillas—but over most of our body, these hairs are so tiny that they are almost invisible.

Scientists believe that humans lost their heavy coat because of their special cooling system. Humans sweat, and the evaporation of the sweat from the skin cools the body. Modern humans have around 3 million sweat glands, more than any other mammal.

"INVISIBLE" HAIRS

Close-up of "invisible" hairs on modern child's arm.

Were early hominids hairy? No one knows for sure. Some artists draw Australo-pithecus *with more fur, some with less.*

Hairy forest-dwelling primates spend most of their time in the shade. But on the savannas, early hominids had to walk and run in the hot sun. Those that had a better way of keeping the body from overheating were able to get more food and raise more offspring. Species with more sweat glands and smaller, finer hairs survived, while those with heavy coats gradually disappeared.

Walking on two legs may not seem very important. It is so natural to us that we take it for granted. But it is actually very unusual. Only birds and a few dinosaurs have been two-legged, and modern humans are the only mammals that walk upright as their usual way of getting around. (Kangaroos use their tail for balance and support, and they usually hop.)

Scientists think that our upright posture has contributed a lot to the way we evolved. It is one reason we became the brainy toolmakers we are today. This is because an upright posture frees the hands from the job of walking.

Once the hands were free, they could be used more and more for tasks such as gathering food, hunting, and fighting enemies. Hands could pick up sticks and stones and use them as tools and weapons. They could even make sticks and stones into better tools and weapons by chipping rocks until the edges were knife-sharp, or by whittling the ends of sticks into points. As time went on, new species of hominids evolved whose hands were more and more nimble.

Upright walking freed hands for other uses.

Once our ancestors left the trees and began using tools, their fingers became shorter and the thumb became longer. The thumb could swivel around at its base and touch the tip of every finger. A thumb like this is called an *opposable* thumb.

Opposable thumb.

If you want to see how useful your opposable thumbs are, try this. Hold your thumbs flat against the sides of your hands. Then try to drink a glass of milk. You will probably find yourself using two hands, the way a squirrel holds a nut.

No hands are as skillful as human hands.

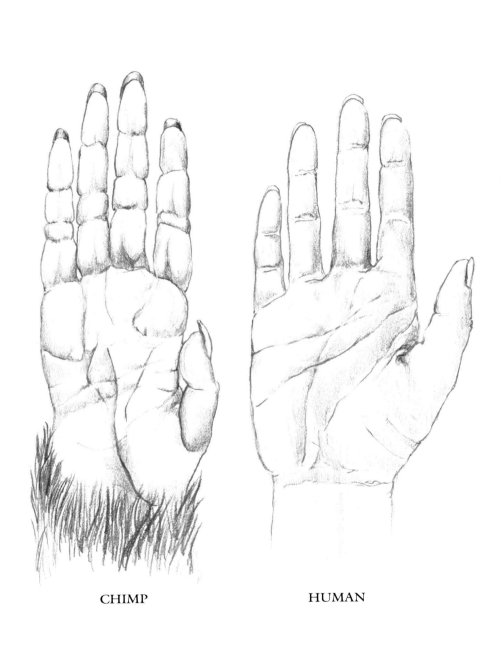

CHIMP HUMAN

A chimp's thumb is shorter than a human's.

The hands of tree-dwelling primates are well suited to grabbing branches. For this, a *hook grip* is used. The thumb lies flat against the side of the hand, and the fingers curl.

Hook grip.

Humans also use the hook grip. It is good for swinging on a jungle gym and for carrying suitcases, among other activities.

But human hands are not limited to the hook grip alone. Two other grips are possible because of our special thumb.

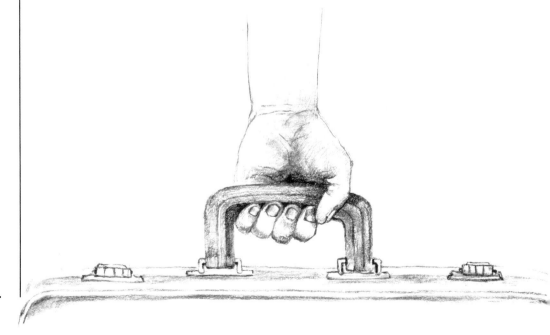

Hook grip.

The *power grip* is used when force is needed: an object is held between the side of the thumb and the palm of the hand.

Power grip.

The *precision grip* is used when accuracy is needed: an object is held between the tip of the index finger and the tip of the thumb.

Precision grip.

Scientists can tell from fossil hand bones that some early humans had thumbs like ours. By studying the tools that early people made, they can also tell that their hands became more skilled as time went on.

Scientists have found fossil bones of a hominid that appeared on earth around 1.5 or 2 million years after Lucy's species had first appeared. *Homo habilis*, or "handy man," is the scientific name for these early humans, but they are also sometimes called habilines (hab-il-EENS).

The habilines were slightly larger than the australopithecines, their brains were bigger, and they had humanlike hands. Habilines made the world's first stone tools, now called pebble tools, or choppers. These were round stones chipped with another stone so that one side had a cutting edge. Pebble tools were probably used for digging, cutting plants and meat, and making other tools out of wood.

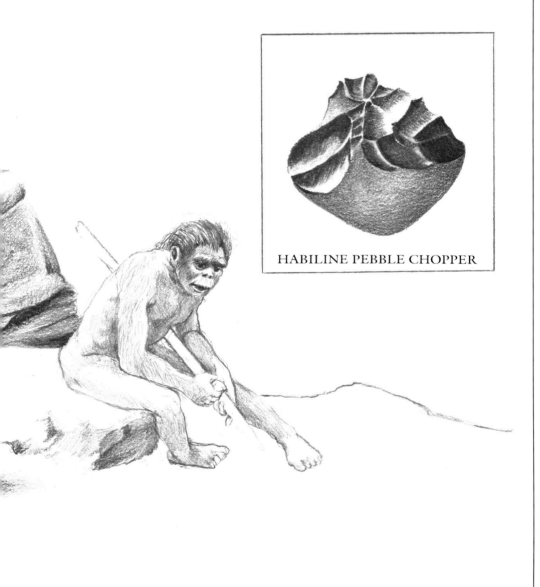

HABILINE PEBBLE CHOPPER

Homo habilis, *2 to 1.5 million years ago.*

A closer relative of modern humans is called *Homo erectus*, whose name means "upright man." *Homo erectus* people had a bigger body and a bigger brain than either the australopithecines or the habilines. Their hands were more skillful also, and their tools were better.

HAND AXE

Instead of only crude pebble tools, *Homo erectus* made pointed hand axes. While a pebble tool could be made with three or four blows from another stone, some of *Homo erectus'* hand axes took more than *sixty* blows to make! Clearly, the hands of *Homo erectus* were about as skillful as our own.

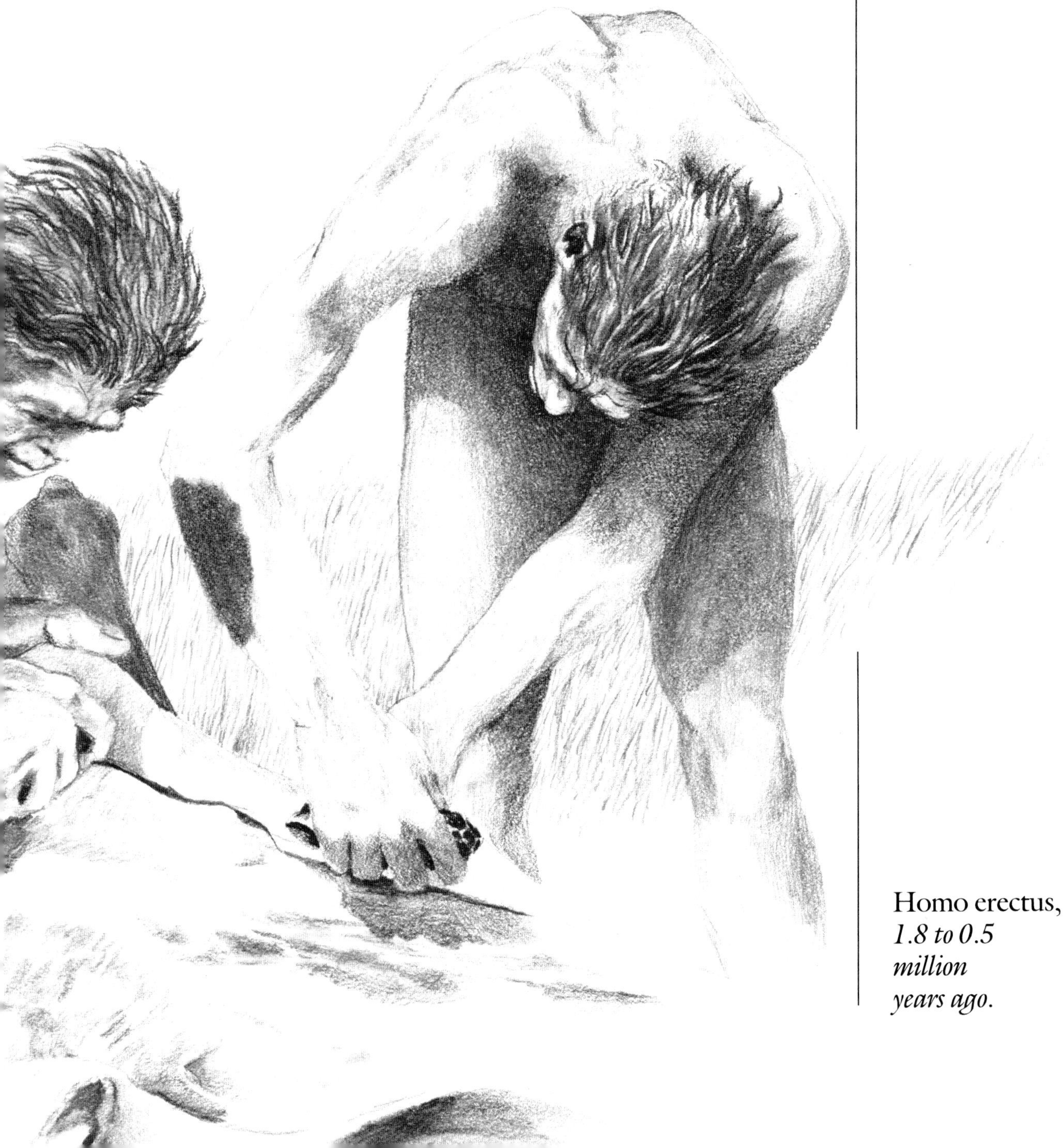

Homo erectus,
*1.8 to 0.5
million
years ago.*

No matter how skilled their hands were, evolving humans also needed the right kind of eyes to help them thrive on the savanna.

Human eyes are placed in the front of the head. Therefore, what one eye sees overlaps with what the other eye sees. The overlap is what gives us our ability to judge distances. This is called stereoscopic vision.

Our stereoscopic vision is something we inherited more or less unchanged from our original tree-dwelling ancestors. They needed good depth vision for leaping from branch to branch. An error of a fraction of an inch could mean serious injury or death.

Zebras' eyes, placed on the sides of the head, are good at detecting movement in a wide circle.

Humans' eyes, placed in the front of the face, are good at focusing on objects.

A simple test can show how your stereoscopic vision helps you use your hands. Draw a dot in the middle of a piece of paper. Lay the paper on a table before you. Then cover one eye and *quickly* place the tip of the pencil on the dot. Try again, covering the other eye. Now do the same thing with both eyes open. If you are like most people, you found it much easier when you used two eyes.

Just by looking with two eyes, we can tell how far or near an object is. So we can easily touch the dot with the pencil, reach out and grab a piece of fruit on a branch, or hit a small animal with a rock or spear.

Try this test to see how stereoscopic vision helps you use your hands.

The partnership of hand and eye gave early humans the ability to use tools with great skill. Our hands—aided by tools—took over some of the work of the jaws and teeth.

Most mammals have large teeth and powerful jaws. They use their mouths to get food and to fight off enemies. The canine teeth are pointed fangs and are used as weapons and to threaten others. When an ape is faced with an enemy, it shows its powerful canine teeth in a snarl. It is safe to assume that our early apelike ancestors also used their teeth like this.

As humans evolved, however, they were more likely to use their hands to fight than their teeth. And instead of seizing food with their teeth, they picked it up in their hands and brought it to their mouths. Thus humans had less and less need for large teeth and powerful jaws.

In addition, humans on the savanna ate foods such as seeds and tough roots. They needed teeth and jaws that could grind these foods. When humans grind tough food, the jaws move from side to side, rather than up and down. Large canine teeth, or fangs, would prevent the jaws from moving sideways.

Albuquerque Academy
MIDDLE SCHOOL LIBRARY
6400 Wyoming Blvd. N.E.
Albuquerque, NM 87109

Modern humans do not have long canine fangs. Our canines are the same size as our incisors, or front teeth. And our chewing teeth themselves are small for our body size. In fact, our chewing teeth are smaller than Lucy's, even though our bodies are much larger than hers.

A change to smaller teeth meant a change in the shape of the jaw and face. Apes' jaws have straight sides. Our jaw is U-shaped, with curved sides.

Apes have large canine teeth, or fangs. Human canine teeth are small.

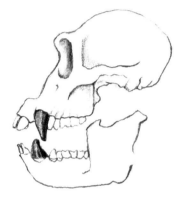

CHIMPANZEE

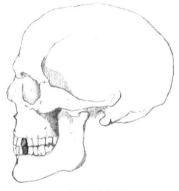

HUMAN

Apes' jaws have straight sides. Human jaws have rounded sides.

CHIMPANZEE UPPER JAW

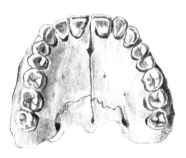

HUMAN UPPER JAW

Most other mammals—including apes—have a long muzzle to make room for the larger teeth. The forehead and chin slope backward. With its smaller teeth and rounded jaws, the human face is flat. The nose may stick out, but the forehead and chin are on the same plane as the mouth.

Looking at the fossil skulls of prehistoric humans, we can see that the muzzle became flatter as time went on. The habiline muzzle is flatter than Lucy's. *Homo erectus*' is flatter still. And this trend continues with later humans, so that today we do not even use the word "muzzle" to describe a human mouth and nose.

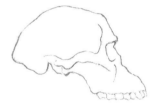
AUSTRALOPITHECINE

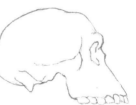
HABILINE

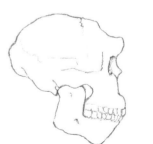
HOMO ERECTUS

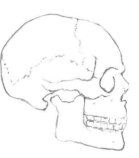
MODERN HUMAN

As time went on, hominid jaws became more rounded, the face became flatter, and the skull higher and rounder.

If you had to choose one feature that makes humans special, it would be our big brain. Humans have a brain that is three to four times larger than the brains of most other mammals of our size.

Parts of our brain control our basic body functions, such as heartbeat, breathing, hunger, and thirst. These functions are regulated by the lower brain—the brain stem and the cerebellum—and the midbrain.

In humans, this area of the brain is very much like that of other animals. Because of this, it is sometimes called the old brain.

The upper brain, or cerebrum, is called the new brain. It is the upper brain that is especially large in humans. And it is the special qualities of the upper brain that make us so intelligent. In humans, the cerebrum is so large that it almost completely covers the old brain like a cap.

39

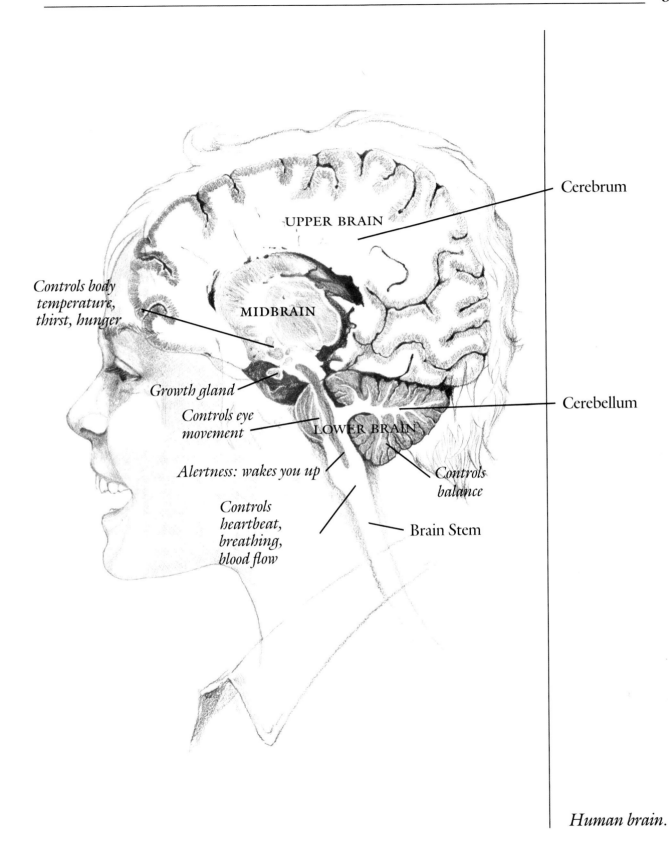

Cerebrum

UPPER BRAIN

*Controls body
temperature,
thirst, hunger*

MIDBRAIN

Growth gland

*Controls eye
movement*

LOWER BRAIN

Cerebellum

Alertness: wakes you up

*Controls
balance*

*Controls
heartbeat,
breathing,
blood flow*

Brain Stem

Human brain.

If the cortex were spread flat, it would be about 20 inches square.

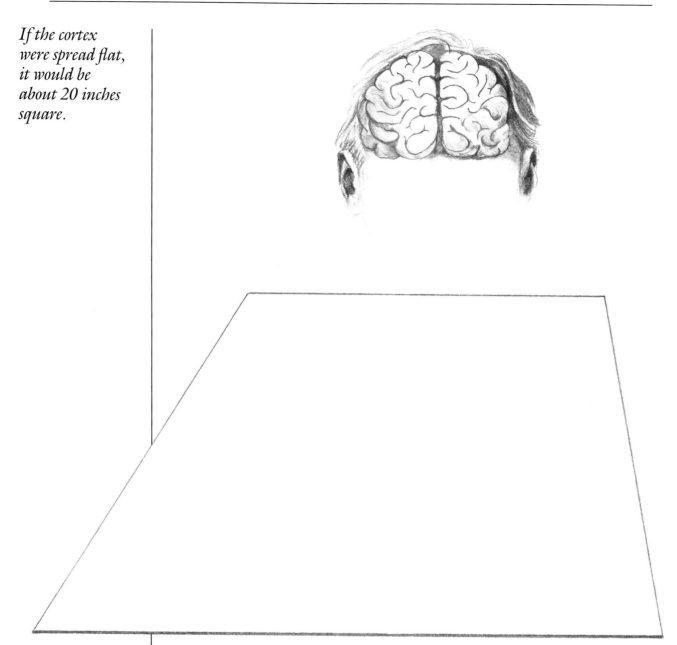

The outer layer of the cerebrum is called the cortex. The cortex is only ⅛ inch thick, but in humans it contains more brain cells than all the rest of the brain put together. Its area is so large that it has to fold in on itself many times just to fit inside our skull. If it were taken out and spread flat, it would be the size of a small tablecloth.

It is not size alone that makes our cortex special. The human cortex has many different parts that have different jobs. Parts of our cortex—the sensory areas—receive information about the world from the eyes, ears, nose, taste buds, and touch nerves.

Other parts of the cortex—the motor areas—control the muscles that help your body move.

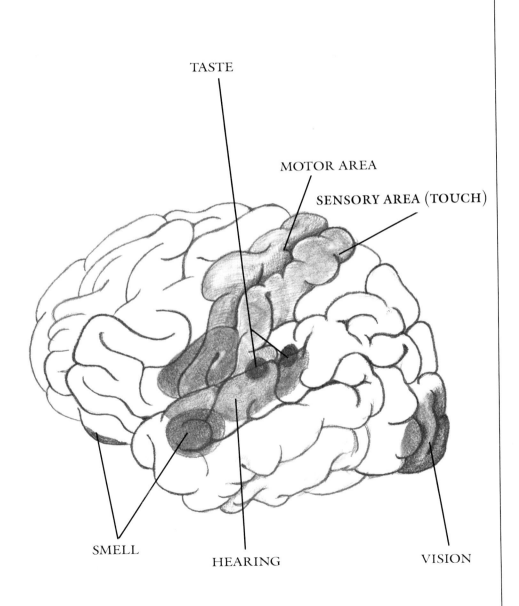

TASTE

MOTOR AREA

SENSORY AREA (TOUCH)

SMELL

HEARING

VISION

Sensory and motor areas of the cortex.

In the brains of other mammals, most of the cortex is made up of these sensory and motor areas. In the human brain, however, there are also very large sections called association areas. Here memories and information are stored. And here billions of connections are made between the nerve cells in one area of the brain and those in another. In the picture of the cortex on the previous page, all the areas in white are association areas.

The association areas make the human brain a very powerful tool for solving problems, remembering, imagining, and planning ahead. So it is typical of humans to react to new situations in many different ways, rather than always in the same way. For example, most mammals cross a river by swimming, but humans may also step on stones, swing on vines, float on a raft, make a bridge, or even build an overhead cable car.

Still other parts of the association areas make it possible for us to communicate with others by using symbols. A symbol is

The association and language areas of the brain make it possible for humans to think and communicate on a high level.

anything—a picture, a gesture, a sound—that stands for something else. Spoken language is a system of sounds that stand for objects or ideas.

A tiny baby cries, and someone tries to figure out what it needs. But after it learns to talk, the baby can say, "I want banana!" Many animals give a warning cry that alerts others to danger, but humans can say, "Hurricane David is approaching the coast from the southwest and will arrive here by midafternoon." You can see that symbolic language can give much more information than mere cries. It can pass on information that cannot be communicated in any other way.

Being able to communicate through language means that humans can accomplish much more as a group than they could ever do as individuals. Groups of humans develop culture—ideas, stories, inventions, and customs—and, through language, they pass on their culture to their children.

People have always wondered why the hominid brain became so large and complex. Some scientists believe the brain began to develop because primates were at a disadvantage on the African savanna. They needed extra intelligence to find food in a challenging environment.

We do not know for sure what early hominids ate on the savanna, but we do know that they could not just live on the grass that was all around, the way grazing animals do. As primates, they needed fruits, seeds, nuts, and edible roots. They also learned to hunt for meat.

Gathering vegetable food on the plains was not as easy as it seems. Early hominids had to predict when different foods would be ripe. They had to remember from year to year where the food was located, and walk long distances to find it. And they had to do all this without being surprised by predators. More intelligent species of prehumans performed these tasks better than the less intelligent, and they were the ones who thrived.

In a similar way, hunting for meat and making tools and weapons stimulated the evolution of intelligence. To make better tools required a more intelligent human. Once those tools were created, they were used best by the most intelligent human species, who then survived, while humans who were not so smart died out.

Early hominids.

Feedback cycle.

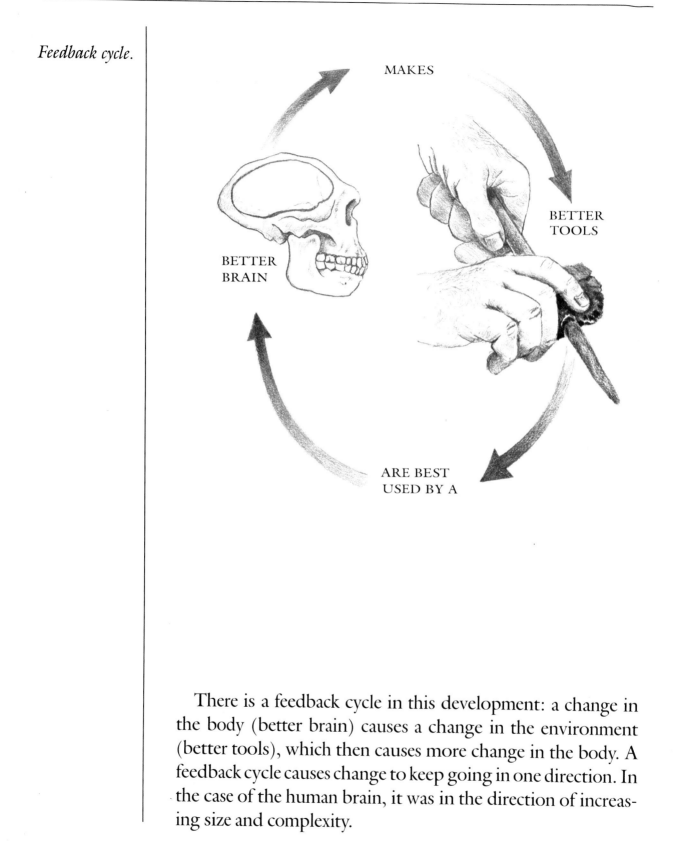

MAKES

BETTER
TOOLS

ARE BEST
USED BY A

BETTER
BRAIN

There is a feedback cycle in this development: a change in the body (better brain) causes a change in the environment (better tools), which then causes more change in the body. A feedback cycle causes change to keep going in one direction. In the case of the human brain, it was in the direction of increasing size and complexity.

From fossil skulls, scientists can trace the development of the human brain. The average brain size for the oldest hominids, the australopithecines, was only about one third the size of a modern human's. The habilines had an average brain a little less than one half the size of a modern person's, and *Homo erectus'* brain was two thirds the size of ours.

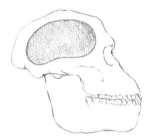

AUSTRALOPITHECINE

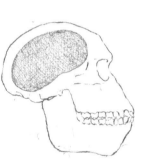

HABILINE

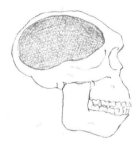

HOMO ERECTUS

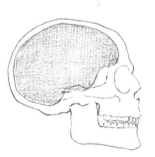

HOMO SAPIENS
(MODERN HUMAN)

Average brain size.

Brain size is only one measure of intelligence. Evidence of culture in the form of fossil tools and the remains of campsites is another.

For the australopithecines, there is no evidence of tool use, although they may have used wooden digging sticks, which did not leave fossils. For the habilines, there are plentiful examples of stone tools. For big-brained *Homo erectus*, there is evidence of still more culture.

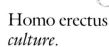

Homo erectus
culture.

Homo erectus people not only made better tools than the smaller-brained habilines. They also invented the use of fire, used clever hunting strategies, ate meat as a regular part of their diet, and had campsites to which they returned again and again.

Homo erectus people were so successful that they expanded their territory across several continents, even moving into colder climates. Their fossils are found not only in Africa, but also in Asia, including Indonesia.

Following *Homo erectus,* new species of humans evolved that were even more intelligent and inventive. Around the time that *Homo erectus* began to disappear, several ancient forms of our own species, *Homo sapiens*—which means "wise, or intelligent, man"—sprang up.

By 150,000 years ago, a group called *Homo sapiens neander-thalensis,* or the Neanderthals, lived in what is now Europe and western Asia. Neanderthals looked different from the way we do, but they were quite intelligent. Although they probably did not have advanced spoken language, they did have large brains. In fact, the brains of some Neanderthals were slightly larger than some brains of our own species.

Neanderthals made improved stone tools, made clothing from animal skins, built huts of branches and skins, hunted large game, cared for the sick, and held ceremonies to bury their dead.

Neanderthal culture.

Living at the same time as the Neanderthals were members of our own species, modern *Homo sapiens*. There were modern humans in many parts of the world. These people left behind amazing works of art: paintings of animals on cave walls, statues carved from stone and antlers, engravings on stones that may have been the first way of keeping records.

Prehistoric Homo sapiens *culture.*

Some scientists think that *Homo erectus* and the Neanderthals had simple language. No one knows for sure. But it seems certain that prehistoric modern *Homo sapiens* had symbolic language because they used symbols in their art.

After the Neanderthals died out around 30,000 years ago, our own species lived on. Of all the species and subspecies of hominids that have lived in the past 3.5 million years, modern *Homo sapiens* is the only one that still survives.

All humans alive today are members of this same species. In different parts of the world, humans developed differences in skin color, hair texture, and body size and shape. But these are surface variations only, mostly adaptations to extremes of climate.

Are our bodies still evolving? In a few thousand years, will humans be different from the way we are now? Some people wonder if our foreheads will bulge out to make room for an even larger brain, or if our legs will become small and useless as we get around more and more in cars and planes.

These are fascinating ideas, but they are probably not true. Our bodies and brains have changed hardly at all from 30,000 years ago, when members of our species were hunting woolly mammoths. And scientists say that very few, if any, changes are taking place in humans today.

Our bodies have not changed, but our culture is constantly changing. It has been only 10,000 or 12,000 years since the hunter-gatherer culture of early *Homo sapiens* was largely replaced by the settled life of farmers. Ten or twelve thousand years may seem like a long time to us, but compared to the whole of human evolution, it is short: less than $1/300$ of all the time that the australopithecines, the habilines, and *Homo erectus* existed.

In this brief time, all of modern culture has evolved. Humans learned to grow crops and breed animals. They built the first villages and towns, made tools and weapons out of metal, and invented writing.

Later, people formed nations and governments, invented the printing press, and entered the age of science. In the last two hundred years, our culture has changed more than in all the past put together.

From a few wandering groups of prehistoric people, our population has grown to billions, and it is still growing. Now humans live almost everywhere on earth, and even survive for periods in space. Inventions such as rockets and computers seem light-years beyond the simple stone implements of our ancestors.

Yet all human history had its beginnings many millions of years ago, when the trees in Africa began to give way to the grasses, starting a process of evolution that gave us the unusual body and amazing brain that are ours today.

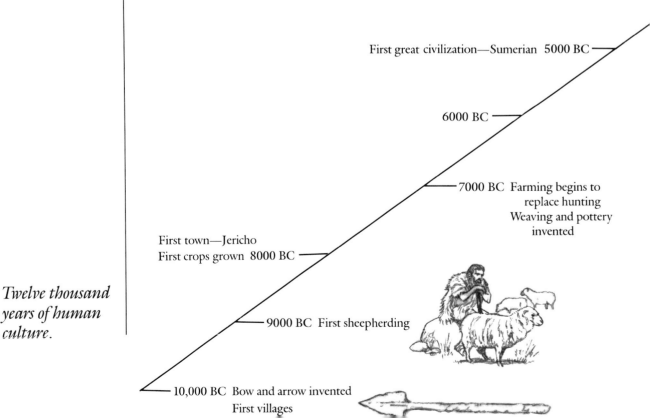

First great civilization—Sumerian 5000 BC

6000 BC

7000 BC Farming begins to replace hunting
Weaving and pottery invented

First town—Jericho
First crops grown 8000 BC

Twelve thousand years of human culture.

9000 BC First sheepherding

10,000 BC Bow and arrow invented
First villages

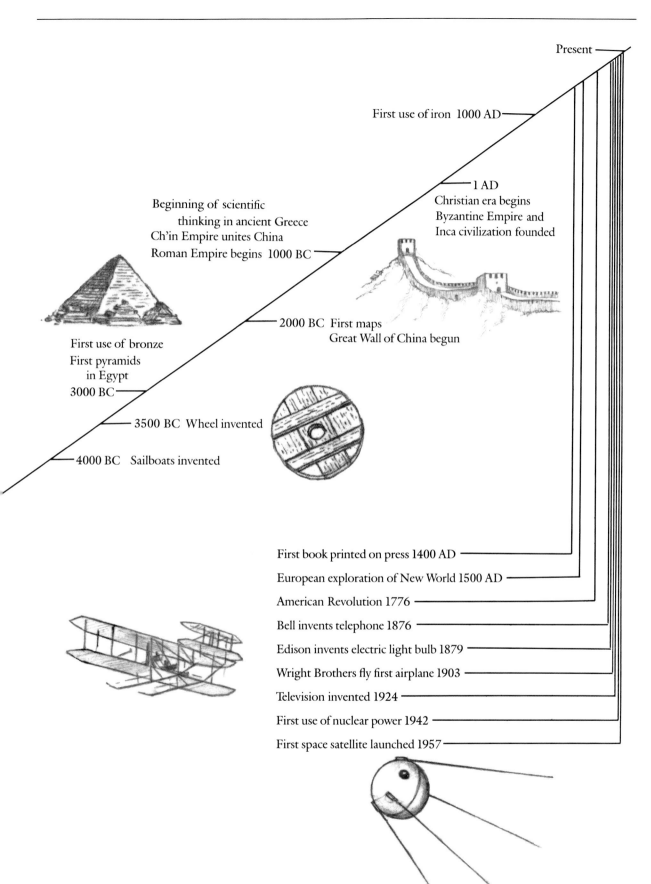

Present

First use of iron 1000 AD

1 AD
Christian era begins
Byzantine Empire and
Inca civilization founded

Beginning of scientific
thinking in ancient Greece
Ch'in Empire unites China
Roman Empire begins 1000 BC

2000 BC First maps
Great Wall of China begun

First use of bronze
First pyramids
in Egypt
3000 BC

3500 BC Wheel invented

4000 BC Sailboats invented

First book printed on press 1400 AD

European exploration of New World 1500 AD

American Revolution 1776

Bell invents telephone 1876

Edison invents electric light bulb 1879

Wright Brothers fly first airplane 1903

Television invented 1924

First use of nuclear power 1942

First space satellite launched 1957

Who's Who Among the Hominids

AUSTRALOPITHECINES (os-TRAL-oh-PITH-uh-seens)

The first hominids. Mostly vegetarian gatherers, with small amount of hunting. Probably used only sticks as tools.

Included three types: *Australopithecus afarensis* (Lucy's species, the oldest australopithecine); *Australopithecus africanus* (similar to Lucy, but brain a little larger); *Australopithecus robustus* and *Australopithecus boisei* (later, more heavily built species).

HOMO HABILIS (HOE-moe HAB-i-lis), or habilines

Similar in appearance to the australopithecines, but had a larger brain and flatter face. Made first tools from rocks. Actively hunted. Probably made temporary campsites.

HOMO ERECTUS (HOE-moe eh-REK-tus)

Body larger than that of *Homo habilis*, with larger brain and smaller teeth. Made more complex stone tools, used fire, built shelters, hunted large game. First hominid to migrate to colder climates.

ARCHAIC *HOMO SAPIENS* (are-KAY-ik HOE-moe SAY-pee-enz)
Ancient, or early, forms of our own species.

HOMO SAPIENS NEANDERTHALENSIS (HOE-moe SAY-pee-enz
nee-AND-er-thal-EN-sis), or Neanderthals

A distinct type of *Homo sapiens* in Europe and the Middle East. Large
brain, body skeleton like ours, skull heavy, with strong brow ridges.
Made advanced stone tools, animal-skin clothing, cave dwellings and
huts, burials. Hunted large game.

HOMO SAPIENS (HOE-moe SAY-pee-enz), or modern human
beings. (*Homo sapiens* found in France are called Cro-Magnon people.)

Large brain in high rounded skull, no brow ridges. Prehistoric *Homo
sapiens* painted cave art, made complex tools such as needles, awls, and
harpoons, may have made primitive calendars. *Homo sapiens* live all over
the world and survive today as modern humans.

When They Lived

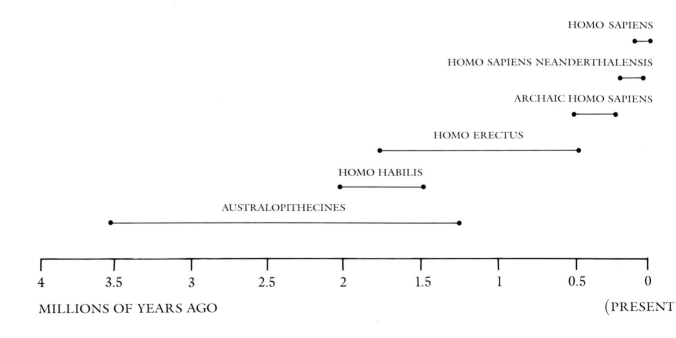

HOMO SAPIENS

HOMO SAPIENS NEANDERTHALENSIS

ARCHAIC HOMO SAPIENS

HOMO ERECTUS

HOMO HABILIS

AUSTRALOPITHECINES

| 4 | 3.5 | 3 | 2.5 | 2 | 1.5 | 1 | 0.5 | 0 |

MILLIONS OF YEARS AGO (PRESENT

Why They Died Out

Why did all the species of hominids die out except for our own, *Homo sapiens*? No one knows for sure. Some species may have died out because they could not adapt to changes in climate or food supply.

But it is more likely that earlier species lost out in competition with later species. Some species may have been killed off by later ones. Or later species may have taken over the territory of the earlier ones, preventing them from getting food and causing their numbers to dwindle.

Some scientists believe that later species could have bred with the species they replaced. If that is true, some Neanderthal and/or *Homo erectus* genes may still be in our bodies today.

Index

JOANNA COLE is a former elementary school teacher and librarian, letters correspondent for *Newsweek,* and senior editor for Doubleday Books for Young Readers. She is now a full-time writer specializing in books for children, many of which have been American Library Association Notable Children's Books of the Year.

Joanna Cole lives in New York City with her husband and their daughter.